Instant RESS Implementation How-to

Take your responsive websites to the next level with server-side components

Chip Lambert

BIRMINGHAM - MUMBAI

Instant RESS Implementation How-to

First published: March 2013

Production Reference: 1200313

Published by Packt Publishing Ltd.
Livery Place
35 Livery Street
Birmingham B3 2PB, UK.

ISBN 978-1-84969-692-0

www.packtpub.com

Credits

Author
Chip Lambert

Reviewer
Anders Andersen

Acquisition Editor
Martin Bell

Commissioning Editor
Priyanka S

Technical Editor
Kaustubh S. Mayekar

Project Coordinator
Joel Goveya

Proofreader
Aaron Nash

Production Coordinator
Prachali Bhiwandkar

Cover Work
Prachali Bhiwandkar

Cover Image
Sheetal Aute

About the Author

Chip Lambert has been creating websites ever since his high schools days, and when he started creating websites, he began with fantasy sport websites. In addition to this 18 years of HTML experience, he has 13 years of experience with PHP and MySQL development. He is currently serving as Director of Applications Development at Bluefield College, where he also teaches HTML5 and CSS3 classes. You can follow him on Twitter @chiplambert.

I would like to thank my beautiful and loving wife, Kelley, for her support over the years on my many projects; I love you! My sweet little pumpkin, Kaitlyn, for sacrificing "daddy time" during the writing of this book; Daddy loves you with all his heart. I would also like to thank my parents; I love you both dearly, and Dad, I miss you and wish you could have seen this.

And, last but not least, I would like to thank David Montgomery-Blake and David Wyand, who each played their own part in getting me introduced to the great folks at Packt Publishing!

About the Reviewer

Anders Andersen is a web developer who specializes in mobile and responsive web development and has been involved in building many of Scandinavia's largest web sites. He has worked for many years as a product manager at Mobiletech, where he and the team built and maintained a successful mobile web solution. He has also been writing and speaking at conferences about building websites that work well for mobile.

He holds a Master of Computer Science from La Trobe University in Melbourne and works as a consultant for Valtech in Stockholm, Sweden. Follow him on Twitter `@andmag`.

www.PacktPub.com

Support files, eBooks, discount offers and more

You might want to visit www.PacktPub.com for support files and downloads related to your book.

Did you know that Packt offers eBook versions of every book published, with PDF and ePub files available? You can upgrade to the eBook version at www.PacktPub.com and as a print book customer, you are entitled to a discount on the eBook copy. Get in touch with us at service@packtpub.com for more details.

At www.PacktPub.com, you can also read a collection of free technical articles, sign up for a range of free newsletters and receive exclusive discounts and offers on Packt books and eBooks.

http://PacktLib.PacktPub.com

Do you need instant solutions to your IT questions? PacktLib is Packt's online digital book library. Here, you can access, read and search across Packt's entire library of books.

Why Subscribe?

- ► Fully searchable across every book published by Packt
- ► Copy and paste, print and bookmark content
- ► On demand and accessible via web browser

Free Access for Packt account holders

If you have an account with Packt at www.PacktPub.com, you can use this to access PacktLib today and view nine entirely free books. Simply use your login credentials for immediate access.

Table of Contents

Preface

Mobile Web is exploding, and this is in large part due to the rise of smartphones, bringing full-featured browsers to the masses, right there in the palms of their hands. Gone are the days when visitors would come to your website through their desktop or laptop computer. Nowadays, your website can get visitors from a laptop, desktop, phone, tablet, or even their television. Do you believe that your site looks the same on all those platforms? More than likely the answer is no. Different screen sizes could make your site look a mess. If you use Flash for anything, more than likely the user will not be able to interact with it. How can you take all these different scenarios into account and make sure your website or web application is fully functional to a visitor, no matter the means they used to get there?

Responsive web design is a method that will allow you to have your website appearance and features change based on the platform the visitor is viewing your site on. This is typically done through JavaScript and CSS.

Unfortunately, there is a problem with standard responsive web design. The main one being the sites that can be large in size, depending on the number of checks and requests being performed and thus leading to longer load times for your site or application. Also, sometimes web developers will create a custom site for mobile devices and redirect them there. This could fail though, and the user could still be stuck with the full-blown website on their phone.

To make things easier, faster, and more reliable, we are going to use RESS, or responsive design and server-side components. That's quite a mouthful! We will use PHP to assist some of the standard responsive design techniques and serve the website all on one URL, rather than sending our visitor to m.example.com or the like. By leveraging PHP's server-side power, we can speed things up a bit and even do some things that aren't usually done easily with standard responsive design.

This book will give you a basic understanding of RESS. We will make a simple site that shows some capabilities of RESS and along the way show you some other tricks and tips you can use in your day-to-day developing.

Let's get started and may all your code be bug free!

What this book covers

Setting up your development environment (Simple) will get your workstation ready for the book.

Getting started with PHP (Simple) will discuss the project and the code we'll write and use.

Using responsive web design (Simple) will give a brief overview of responsive web design and how to use it.

Getting started with Modernizr (Simple) will explain how to get started with the feature detection library, Modernizr.

Finding your visitors with Modernizr (Intermediate) will help you to use Modernizr for geolocation support detection.

Checking for web storage with Modernizr (Intermediate) will discuss using Modernizr to see if the device supports HTML's web storage.

Getting started with WURFL (Intermediate) will enable you to use the WURFL Cloud service from ScientiaMobile for device detection.

Using WURFL to check for Apple devices (Intermediate) will provide guidance for checking to see if the visitor is using an iOS device.

Bringing responsive design with PHP (Simple) will enable you to start putting all the pieces together for your site.

Laying out our page with RESS (Intermediate) will enable you to use Modernizr and PHP to start laying out your website.

Displaying images (Intermediate) will teach you how to use PHP to display different sized images.

Getting visitor feedback (Advanced) will help us to display a form that is geared towards the device the user is using.

Wrapping it up (Simple) will summarize your work and guide you where to go from here.

What you need for this book

In this book, we will be writing code, so you will need at least a text editor. I recommend a full PHP IDE, such as Eclipse PDT or Zend Studio. In this book, we will be using Aptana Studio 3, a free Eclipse-based IDE that supports PHP, HTML5, CSS, JavaScript, and several other languages.

It is also in your best interests to have access to a PHP-based server, so you can test your code. In the first recipe, we will go through installing XAMPP, a full PHP-based web server solution, right there on your workstation. No additional server equipment needed!

Who this book is for

This book will give a basic understanding of RESS along with some very basic standard responsive web design techniques. We will be using PHP, HTML5, JavaScript, and CSS to accomplish our goals, so it is assumed that you have a good understanding of these languages and technologies. This book will not serve as an introduction to them.

Conventions

In this book, you will find a number of styles of text that distinguish between different kinds of information. Here are some examples of these styles, and an explanation of their meaning.

Code words in text are shown as follows: "Go ahead and set this to the `htdocs` folder of your XAMPP installation."

A block of code is set as follows:

```
#content {
    width: 95%;
    margin: 0em 0em 1em 0em;
    background-color: red;
    color: white;
}
```

New terms and **important words** are shown in bold. Words that you see on the screen, in menus or dialog boxes for example, appear in the text like this: "Make your choice and then click on **OK**".

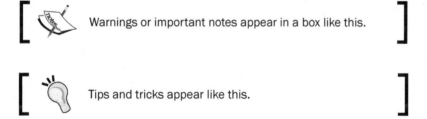

Warnings or important notes appear in a box like this.

Tips and tricks appear like this.

Reader feedback

Feedback from our readers is always welcome. Let us know what you think about this book—what you liked or may have disliked. Reader feedback is important for us to develop titles that you really get the most out of.

To send us general feedback, simply send an e-mail to `feedback@packtpub.com`, and mention the book title via the subject of your message.

If there is a book that you need and would like to see us publish, please send us a note in the **SUGGEST A TITLE** form on www.packtpub.com or e-mail suggest@packtpub.com.

If there is a topic that you have expertise in and you are interested in either writing or contributing to a book, see our author guide on www.packtpub.com/authors.

Customer support

Now that you are the proud owner of a Packt book, we have a number of things to help you to get the most from your purchase.

Downloading the example code

You can download the example code files for all Packt books you have purchased from your account at http://www.PacktPub.com. If you purchased this book elsewhere, you can visit http://www.PacktPub.com/support and register to have the files e-mailed directly to you.

Errata

Although we have taken every care to ensure the accuracy of our content, mistakes do happen. If you find a mistake in one of our books—maybe a mistake in the text or the code—we would be grateful if you would report this to us. By doing so, you can save other readers from frustration and help us improve subsequent versions of this book. If you find any errata, please report them by visiting http://www.packtpub.com/support, selecting your book, clicking on the **errata submission form** link, and entering the details of your errata. Once your errata are verified, your submission will be accepted and the errata will be uploaded on our website, or added to any list of existing errata, under the Errata section of that title. Any existing errata can be viewed by selecting your title from http://www.packtpub.com/support.

Piracy

Piracy of copyright material on the Internet is an ongoing problem across all media. At Packt, we take the protection of our copyright and licenses very seriously. If you come across any illegal copies of our works, in any form, on the Internet, please provide us with the location address or website name immediately so that we can pursue a remedy.

Please contact us at copyright@packtpub.com with a link to the suspected pirated material.

We appreciate your help in protecting our authors, and our ability to bring you valuable content.

Questions

You can contact us at questions@packtpub.com if you are having a problem with any aspect of the book, and we will do our best to address it.

Instant RESS Implementation How-to

Welcome to *Instant RESS Implementation How-to*. This book will get you started on the path of using responsive web design with PHP to make your website look at its best on any platform your visitors could possibly use.

Setting up your development environment (Simple)

In this section, I will help you get your workstation set up so that you can follow along with the code in this book. You can read the code all day long, but to truly understand and grasp what the code is doing, it is best to read the code, and then type it and see how it executes.

Getting ready

To get our development environment going, we will be installing Aptana Studio 3 for our IDE and XAMPP for our web server environment. Both of these packages exist for Windows, Mac, and Linux, so no matter what your OS of choice is, you will be able to follow along. Also, they both are free.

How to do it...

First, we will install XAMPP.

XAMPP is a full-blown web server package. It includes Apache, PHP, MySQL, Tomcat, Perl, phpMyAdmin, and more.

The first thing we need to do is download XAMPP. You can find the installation file for your operating system at `http://www.apachefriends.org/en/xampp.html`. I recommend using the installer for Windows, instead of using the Zip file method.

This installation is pretty straightforward.

For Windows, follow these steps:

1. Double-click on the installation, and you will be asked to select a language. Make your choice and then click on **OK**.

2. If you are using Windows Vista or Windows 7, and User Account Control or UAC is enabled, you will be presented with a warning that some of the functionality may be limited if you install XAMPP to the `Program Files` directory. Click on **OK**.

3. Another warning may pop up stating that you need to install the Microsoft Visual C++ 2008 redistributable package. Clicking on **Yes** will open a web page on the Microsoft Download Center, where you can download this package. Do so and then continue the XAMPP installation.

4. Click on **Next**, and then you can decide which features you want installed with your installation. For now, just leave the defaults as is and click on **Next**.

5. The default directory should be fine, so leave it as is and click on **Install**.

6. The installation itself will take several minutes; once it is finished, click on **Finish** on the screen that pops up.

7. You will then be presented with a screen that will inform you that all the services can controlled through a XAMPP Control Panel. It will ask you if you want to open that screen now, and then click on **Yes**.

8. On the **Control Panel** screen, you will be able to start and stop all the services that XAMPP installed. By default, these services may be off, so for now, let's turn on Apache by clicking on the **Start** button next to it.

For installation on Mac OS, simply download the `.DMG` file, open it up, and drag the folder into the `Applications` directory. After this, open up the XAMPP Control Panel (from the `Applications` folder of XAMPP) and start Apache, MySQL, and ProFTPD. You may have to do this each time you restart your Mac.

To verify that everything was installed correctly and is working, open up your web browser and go to `http://localhost`. You should see a screen similar to the following screenshot:

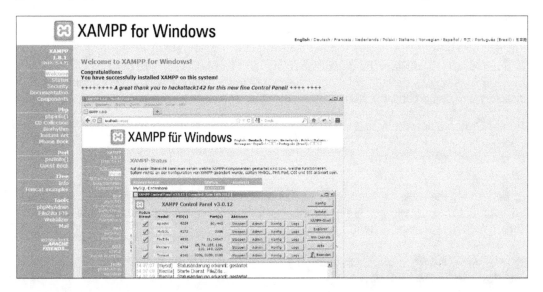

Congratulations, you now have a fully functional web server installed with PHP support! If you do not see this screen, make sure you've started the Apache service and followed all the installation steps correctly.

Now, we will install Aptana Studio.

Aptana Studio 3 can be downloaded from `http://www.aptana.com/products/studio3/download`. Currently, there exists Aptana Studio 2 and 3. We will be using Aptana Studio 3 for this book, so be sure that is the one you download.

For Windows, follow these steps:

1. Double-click on the installer file, and select **Next** to get the installation started.

2. Choose **I Agree** to accept the license agreement.

3. The default directory should be fine, as should the default programs group, so hit **Next** on these two screens.

4. The installer will now prompt you to choose what file extensions Aptana should be the default editor for. Leave the default settings on here. You can change it later in the IDE if you wish to. Click on **Next**.

5. Click on **Install** to start the installation. Once the installation is finished, click on **Next** and then on **Close**.

For Mac users, again download the .DMG file, open it, then drag it into the Applications folder.

After you have it installed, go ahead and open it. The first thing you will be presented with is a screen asking you to set up your default workspace directory. Go ahead and set this to the htdocs folder of your XAMPP installation. For Windows users, this is c:\xampp\htdocs (provided you kept the default directory) and for Mac is /Applications/XAMPP/htdocs. This way, by default, all of our projects are in the Apache web server documents directory and can be easily tested without having to move files back and forth.

That's it. You are now ready to learn RESS!

How it works...

By performing the previous steps, we have set up a full-blown web server on our development environment that will allow us faster development time by not having to upload to a remote server each time we wish to test.

There's more

There are several other PHP IDEs out there, such as Zend Studio, PHP Storm, and a host of others. If you already use Eclipse for other purposes, Aptana Studio can be downloaded as an Eclipse plugin (requires Eclipse 3.5 or higher). For the purposes of this book, we will be using the stand-alone version of the software.

XAMPP security

A very important note about XAMPP is that while it appears, it would be easy to use to set up a full-blown web server; it is not recommended from a security standpoint to use XAMPP in a production server environment. It should only be used for development and testing purposes.

XAMPP on Mac OS

XAMPP for Mac is still listed as being in beta. Please take that into consideration before installing it on your system. Other MAMP solutions exist, and those would serve the same purpose of XAMPP for this book. One that is highly recommended is conveniently known as MAMP and can be found at http://www.mamp.info/en/index.html.

Also, a note about the `htdocs` folder of XAMPP is that, by default, it is owned by root, and therefore, it is read-only. If you encounter an error while starting Aptana, you may need to change permissions on this folder. To do so:

1. Click on the folder in **Finder** and then choose the **Get Info from the File** menu.
2. Click on the triangle next to **Sharing & Permissions** to display permissions for the selected file or folder.
3. Click on the lock and authenticate with an administrator account.
4. Use the menus next to users and groups to change the permissions.
5. When you're finished, close the **Info** window.

Finding more support

For support on installing either of these software packages, please see their respective websites.

Getting started with PHP (Simple)

In this topic, we will discuss the website we are going to make, go over how to create a project in Aptana Studio 3, and talk about the libraries we are going to use.

First, let's talk about the website we are going to make. We are going to make a simple website that will showcase the features we learn in this book. It is nothing spectacularly grand, however, it will hopefully give you the basis you need to implement RESS in your own websites and web applications.

Along the way, we will use a few third-party libraries and APIs to make our lives easier and keep us from having to create our own. Throughout this book, we will use Modernizr, a JavaScript library for feature detection and WURFL, a device detection API that is a little safer to use instead of just standard user-agent detection.

Let's go ahead and create the initial project in Aptana Studio that we will use, and see what our folder structure will look like.

Getting ready

Go ahead and open up Aptana Studio if it is not already open.

How to do it...

Follow these steps:

1. Choose **File | New | PHP Project**. You should see the window appear, as shown in the following screenshot:

You can name the project whatever you wish; just keep in mind that the project name will also serve as the URL when you go to test in your browser.

2. By clicking on **Finish**, you create your first project in Aptana Studio.

    Let's go ahead and create our base folder structure. This allows us to go ahead and get organized before we start adding code.

3. You have two options for creating the folder structure. You can go directly into the project folder through Windows Explorer or Mac Finder and create the following structure, or you can right-click and choose **New | Folder** in the area called **App Explorer** on the left-hand side of the screen in Aptana Studio. Creating them outside the program is a bit faster, and you will then see them appear in Aptana Studio.

4. Go ahead and create some directories so that your screen will look like the following screenshot:

5. You will see that I have created some files as well. You can do that by right-clicking on the folder in this view and choosing **New | File**. Go ahead and create the files as well. I'll explain these folders and file in the next section.

How it works...

Now, I'll explain the folders we just created:

- ▶ css: This folder holds all of our style sheets

- ▶ images: This folder holds all of the images we will use on the site

- ▶ includes: This folder holds all of the PHP code that will be included in our project, such as classes and other files

- ▶ js: This folder is for all of our JavaScript files and libraries

- ▶ WURFL: This folder holds the code for the WURFL API

- ▶ header.inc/footer.inc: This folder is used for separating code out for maintainability and allows us to use header and footer files

- ▶ Index.php: This, of course, is our main PHP file

Using responsive web design (Simple)

In this section, we will discuss responsive web design and how to start implementing it.

Responsive web design is typically done on the client side with media queries, which is an extension of the media rule of CSS that was introduced in CSS 2. Again, this is all done on the client, which means that, eventually, depending on how many HTTP requests you are performing, the site can have several MBs of overhead. Depending on the device, connection, and so on, this could have an impact on the speed of your site or application.

With media queries, you can have the page use different CSS styles, depending on a number of factors, but the most used one is the device's screen width. Typically, you want to use a fluid grid concept for layout; this means using em and percentages in lieu of straight pixel values. Images are also usually flexible and sized in relative units to keep them within their container.

I believe that's enough background information; let's see all this in action.

Getting ready

Create a new project in Aptana Studio; call it whatever you wish. I recommend using the `Web Project` template this time instead of the `PHP Project` template we used previously.

Once you have created the project, it should have created a template for you, `index.html`. Go ahead and add two more files named `mobile.css` and `desktop.css`. These two files will hold our design information.

How to do it...

Okay, now that we have our project and files set up, it's time to start writing some code. To do so, follow these steps:

1. Open up `mobile.css` and type the following:

   ```
   #content {
     width: 95%;
     margin: 0em 0em 1em 0em;
     background-color: red;
     color: white;
   }
   ```

2. Now open up `desktop.css` and type the following:

   ```
   #content {
     width: 95%;
     margin: 0em 0em 1em 0em;
   ```

```
    background-color: black;
    color: white;
}
```

3. So, we now have our CSS finished; let's see it in action. Open `index.html` and type the following:

```html
<!DOCTYPE html>
    <head>
        <meta name="viewport" content="width=device-width" />
            <meta http-equiv="Content-Type" content="text/html;
charset=utf-8" />
            <title>Responsive Web Design Example</title>
            <link type="text/css" rel="stylesheet" media="only screen
and (max-device-width: 480px)" href="css/mobile.css" />
            <link type="text/css" rel="stylesheet" media="only screen
and (min-device-width: 1024px)" href="css/desktop.css" />
    </head>
    <body>

        <div id="content">
        Hello World!
        </div>
</body>
</html>
```

4. Now if you open this page in your desktop/laptop browser, you will see the following screenshot:

5. Just as we expected, we see the black background we specified for the standard browser version. Now let's see it from a mobile point of view, as shown in the following screenshot:

How it works...

Let's take a look at the code:

1. The two CSS files contain some real basic CSS styling, so we won't cover them.

```
<!DOCTYPE HTML PUBLIC "-//W3C//DTD HTML 4.01 Transitional//EN"
"http://www.w3.org/TR/html4/loose.dtd">
<html xmlns="http://www.w3.org/1999/xhtml">
    <head>
```

2. This code is just your basic opening HTML code and is auto-generated by Aptana Studio. The next piece is important for iOS devices:

```
<meta name="viewport" content="width=device-width" />
```

3. This code forces the iOS browsers to zoom in. If it is not there, occasionally the iPhone or iPad will render the page fully zoomed out, and your code won't look right.

```
<link type="text/css" rel="stylesheet" media="only screen and
(max-device-width: 480px)" href="mobile.css" />
 <link type="text/css" rel="stylesheet" media="only screen and
(min-device-width: 1024px)" href="desktop.css" />
```

4. Here, we are linking our CSS files and performing a media query at the same time. In the first line, we are saying that if the device screen is 480 px wide or less, load our mobile style sheet, and then in the next line, we are saying if our device is at minimum 1024 px, then load our desktop style sheet.

```
<div id="content">
Hello World!
</div>
```

5. And finally, we are simply loading our content using the classic "Hello World" programming example.

There's more...

There are several options you can check for in a media query. In this very basic example, we just checked the device width; you can also check orientation, aspect ratio, resolution, and much more. You can see what all you can check with media queries on the CSS section of the W3C website at `http://www.w3.org/TR/css3-mediaqueries/`.

Tools

There are several tools you can use to test the way your site looks on mobile devices. I recommend Screenfly (`http://quirktools.com/screenfly/`). You can see how your device looks on iOS devices, various Android phones and tablets, and even on 720p and 1080p TV sets.

Also, if you use Chrome, there is an extension called Window Resizer that allows you to mimic mobile and tablet screen widths to test CSS.

Of course, it is always best to check on the devices itself, but this tool can help you out when no device is available.

Getting started with Modernizr (Simple)

From the Modernizr website:

Modernizr is a small JavaScript library that detects the availability of native implementations for next-generation web technologies, i.e. features that stem from the HTML5 and CSS3 specifications. Many of these features are already implemented in at least one major browser (most of them in two or more), and what Modernizr does is, very simply, tell you whether the current browser has this feature natively implemented or not.

Basically with this library, we can see if the user's browser can support certain features you wish to use on your site. This is important to do, as unfortunately not every browser is created the same. Each one has its own implementation of the HTML5 standard, so some features may be available on Google Chrome but not on Internet Explorer. Using Modernizr is a better alternative to the standard, but it is unreliable, **user agent (UA)** string checking.

Let's begin.

Getting ready

Go ahead and create a new Web Project in Aptana Studio. Once it is set up, go ahead and add a new folder to the project named `js`.

Next thing we need to do is to download the Development Version of Mondernizr from the Modernizr download page (`http://modernizr.com/download/`). You will see options to build your own package. The development version will do until you are ready for production use. As of this writing, the latest version is 2.6.2 and that will be the version we use.

Place the downloaded file into the `js` folder.

How to do it...

Follow these steps:

1. For this exercise, we will simply do a browser test to see if your browser currently supports the HTML5 Canvas element. Type this into a JavaScript file named `canvas.js` and add the following code:

```
if (Modernizr.canvas)
{
var c=document.getElementById("canvastest");
var ctx=c.getContext("2d");

// Create gradient
Var grd=ctx.createRadialGradient(75,50,5,90,60,100);
grd.addColorStop(0,"black");
grd.addColorStop(1,"white");

// Fill with gradient
ctx.fillStyle=grd;
ctx.fillRect(10,10,150,80);
alert("We can use the Canvas element!");
}
else
{
   alert("Canvas Element Not Supported");
}
```

2. Now add the following to `index.html`:

```
<!DOCTYPE html>
    <head>
        <meta http-equiv="Content-Type" content="text/html;
charset=utf-8" />
        <title>Canvas Support Test</title>
        <script src="js/modernizr-latest.js" type="text/
javascript"></script>
    </head>
    <body>
    <canvas id="canvastest" width="200" height="100"
style="border:1px solid #000000">Your browser does not support the
HTML5 canvas tag.</canvas>
    <script src="js/canvas.js">
    </script>
    </body>
</html>
```

3. Let's preview the code and see what we got. The following screenshot is what you should see:

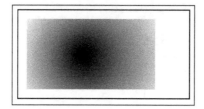

How it works...

What did we just do? Well, let's break it down:

```
<script src="js/modernizr-latest.js" type="text/javascript"></script>
```

Here, we are calling in our Modernizr library that we downloaded previously. Once you do that, Modernizr does some things to your page. It will redo your opening `<html>` tag to something like the following (from Google Chrome):

```
<html class=" js flexbox flexboxlegacy canvas canvastext webgl no-
touch geolocation postmessage websqldatabase indexeddb hashchange
history draganddrop websockets rgba hsla multiplebgs backgroundsize
borderimage borderradius boxshadow textshadow opacity cssanimations
csscolumns cssgradients cssreflections csstransforms csstransforms3d
csstransitions fontface generatedcontent video audio localstorage
sessionstorage webworkers applicationcache svg inlinesvg smil
svgclippaths">
```

This is all the features your browser supports that Modernizr was able to detect.

Next up we have our `<canvas>` element:

```
<canvas id="canvastest" width="200" height="100" style="border:1px
solid #000000">Your browser does not support the HTML5 canvas tag.</
canvas>
```

Here, we are just forming a basic canvas that is 200 x 100 with a black border going around it.

Now for the good stuff in our `canvas.js` file, follow this code snippet:

```
<script>
    if (Modernizr.canvas)
    {
alert("We can use the Canvas element!");
        var c=document.getElementById("canvastest");
        var ctx=c.getContext("2d");

        // Create gradient
        var grd=ctx.createRadialGradient(75,50,5,90,60,100);
        grd.addColorStop(0,"black");
        grd.addColorStop(1,"white");

        // Fill with gradient
        ctx.fillStyle=grd;
        ctx.fillRect(10,10,150,80);

    }
    else
    {
        alert("Canvas Element Not Supported");
    }
</script>
```

In the first part of this snippet, we used an `if` statement to see if the browser supports the Canvas element. If it does support canvas, then we are displaying a JavaScript alert and then filling our canvas element with a black gradient. After that, we have our `else` statement that will alert the user that canvas is not supported on their browser. They will also see the **Your browser does not support the HTML5 canvas tag** message.

That wasn't so bad, was it?

There's more...

I highly recommend reading over the documentation on the Modernizr website so that you can see all the feature tests you can do with this library. We will do a few more practice examples with Modernizr, and of course, it will be a big component of our RESS project later on in the book.

Keeping it efficient

For a production environment, I highly recommend taking the build-a-package approach and only downloading a script that contains the tests you will actually use. This way your script is as small as possible. As of right now, the file we used has every test in it; some you may never use. So, to be as efficient as possible (and we want all the efficiency we can get in mobile development), build your file with the tests you'll use or may use.

Finding your visitors with Modernizr (Intermediate)

We dabbled with the Modernizr library very briefly in the previous topic to test for the canvas element. The canvas element is just one of the features we can check for with this library. In this section, we will look at the geolocation feature of HTML5.

What is geolocation feature you ask? Geolocation allows us to calculate the geographical location of our visitors, providing they allow the website to access it. Thanks to HTML5! Google Maps is a perfect example of a web application using geolocation.

How does this work? The browser taps into the GPS of the phone (if one is present), and uses cell-tower triangulation and other techniques to generate the geographical data. More than likely if a user visits your site on a smartphone, the browser will use the GPS for the best accuracy, providing the GPS radio is on.

Also, as mentioned already, being able to access the geolocation information of your visitors is completely up to them. They have to explicitly allow you this access each time they visit your site. Keep that in mind when making websites that use this information; by that, I mean don't penalize them or cripple their experience on your site or application if they don't share this information with you.

Getting ready

Create a new Web Project in Aptana Studio. If you do not get the `index.html` file automatically created, please create it now. Copy over the `js` folder from the previous project, as we will be using the Modernizr library again.

How to do it...

Follow these steps:

1. In `index.html`, type the following code:

```html
<!DOCTYPE html>
<html>
  <head>
    <meta http-equiv="Content-Type" content="text/html;
charset=utf-8" />
    <title>Canvas Support Test</title>
    <script src="js/modernizr-latest.js" type="text/javascript"></
script>
    <script type="text/javascript">
      function findMe()
      {
      if (Modernizr.geolocation) {
          alert("Geolocation supported!!!");
          navigator.geolocation.getCurrentPosition(showCurrentLoca
tion, errorHandler, {
            enableHighAccuracy : true
          });
        } else {
          alert("Your Browser does not support Geolocation.");
        }
      }
      function showCurrentLocation(position)
      {
          document.getElementById("curlocation").innerHTML =
"Current Latitude : " + position.coords.latitude + " , Current
Longitude : " + position.coords.longitude;
      }
      function errorHandler(error)
      {
          alert("Error while retrieving current position. Error
code: " + error.code + ",Message: " + error.message);
      }
    </script>
  </head>
  <body>
    <div id="main">
      <div id="curlocation">
```

```
            <input type="button" value="Find My Location"
    onclick="findMe()"/>
          </div>
        </div>
      </body>
    </html>
```

2. Save the file and open the project up in your favorite web browser. You should see a simple button that looks like the following screenshot:

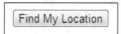

3. Go ahead and click on the button, and you'll see a JavaScript alert stating whether or not you have geolocation in your browser. After the alert and providing nothing happened, you'll see something like the following screenshot (I blacked my info out for obvious reasons):

How it works...

Let's take a look at our code; some of this code repeats from the previous section, so we'll just look at the new stuff:

```
    function findMe()
    {
      if (Modernizr.geolocation) {
        alert("Geolocation supported!!!");
        navigator.geolocation.getCurrentPosition(showCurrentLocati
    on, errorHandler, {
          enableHighAccuracy : true
        });
      } else {
        alert("Your Browser does not support Geolocation.");
      }
    }
```

This piece is in a JavaScript function, which means we can reuse our JavaScript code. First thing we do is assign the `navigator.geolocation` value to a JavaScript variable for later use. We are still checking Modernizr for the geolocation feature. If that returns `true`, then we are displaying our alert, getting the current position through the geolocation API, passing it the `showCurrentLocation` function, and then assigning an error handler. The `enableHighAccuracy` parameter assures that we get the most accurate coordinates for the user. And, finally, we are displaying our alert stating that this browser does not support geolocation.

```
function showCurrentLocation(position)
{
    document.getElementById("curlocation").innerHTML = "Current Latitude
: " + position.coords.latitude + " , Current Longitude : " + position.
coords.longitude;
}
```

This function will display our current location on the screen and is called in our main `findMe()` function.

```
function errorHandler(error)
{       alert("Error while retrieving current position. Error code: " +
error.code + ",Message: " + error.message);
}
```

Here, we are doing our error handling. The three main possible values here are as follows:

- `PositionError.PERMISSION_DENIED`: User did not allow the website to access this information
- `PositionError.UNAVAILABLE`: Unable to determine position
- `PositionError.TIMEOUT`: System timed out on determining the position

You should be sure to account for this in your code, so you can handle these errors gracefully.

There's more...

Geolocation is a great tool we can use on websites and in web applications. You could tailor particular pieces of information to people based on their location; this could be news, ads, and so on. Just be aware that some people don't like to be tracked, so if they are required to submit their location, you might have just lost a user.

Supporting Internet Explorer

Prior to Internet Explorer 9, IE did not support geolocation. However, there is a way you can include those users in this as well and that is with `geoposition.js`, which is an open source JavaScript library that emulates a lot of the geolocation functionality. You can find more information about it at `https://github.com/estebanav/javascript-mobile-desktop-geolocation/`.

Blackberry and Nokia tidbit

Blackberry and Nokia devices include their own geolocation library, and therefore, they may not be compatible with this code.

Checking for web storage with Modernizr (Intermediate)

So, we've checked for canvas support and found the coordinates of our users. Now lets look at another cool feature of HTML5, web storage. What is web storage you say? Web storage is capable of several things. For one, it can be a replacement for session and cookie data, and it can be used to allow access to a sandboxed filesystem. This means, you will be able to read/write files to the storage area.

In this example, we will look at a very basic and crude text editor. We will put some information into a text area and then save/retrieve it through web storage.

Getting ready

Make a new Web Project in Aptana Studio, make sure you have an `index.html` file, and copy over the `js` folder that we used in the previous topics.

How to do it...

Type the following into `index.html`:

```
<!DOCTYPE html>
<html>
  <head>
    <meta http-equiv="Content-Type" content="text/html; charset=utf-8" />
    <title>Webstorage Support Test</title>
    <script src="js/modernizr-latest.js" type="text/javascript"></script>
  </head>
  <body>
    <textarea id="storedtext" width="300" height="300">

    </textarea>
    <script>
      if (Modernizr.localstorage)
      {
        alert("Web Storage found");
        var savedtext = document.getElementById("storedtext");
```

```
            savedtext.value = localStorage.getItem("webStoreTest") || "";
            savedtext.addEventListener("keyup", function () {
                localStorage.setItem("webStoreText", storedtext.value);
            },false)
        }
        else
        {
            alert("Browser does not allow web storage");
        }

    </script>
    </body>
</html>
```

So, this example looks extremely short. The truth is web storage is easy! In my opinion, it is one of the easiest and most powerful features of HTML5. Go ahead and open it up in your browser, and you will see a `textarea` control on the page. Type as much information as you want. Now close the page and reopen it. The text you typed should still be there. If not, double-check your code.

How it works...

Now let's take a look at our code:

```
<script>
    if (Modernizr.localstorage)
    {
        alert("Web Storage found");
```

Again we are doing our Modernizr check for `localstorage` (note that it is `localstorage` and not `webstorage`). Also note that, the JavaScript object is `localStorage`, so be sure to keep the two separate. JavaScript is case-sensitive, so it will give an error if you try to use `localstorage.getItem ("myText")`.

```
    var savedtext = document.getElementById("storedtext");
            savedtext.value = localStorage.getItem("webStoreTest") || "";
```

After our Modernizr check, we establish a few JavaScript variables we will need and assign the `textarea` control to those variables. We then load into those variables anything saved in our web storage field `webStoreTest` so that the initial text of the `textarea` control will equal that field. If nothing exists in `webStoreTest`, then we are assigning it an empty string (`" "`).

```
    savedtext.addEventListener("keyup", function () {
            localStorage.setItem("webStoreTest", storedtext.value);
        },false)
    }
```

After we check it for any text stored in web storage, we start our text-saving function. We are doing that by adding a listener that will detect our keystrokes and save them into our web storage field `webStoreText`. This saving happens automatically with no intervening on our parts.

```
else
{
   alert("Browser does not allow web storage");
}
```

And in our final piece, we display our alert that we do not have web storage functionality in this browser.

There's more...

As mentioned earlier, you can also use this for storing session and cookie information. I highly recommend reading up on how you can do this and implement it in your future projects.

The future of web storage

Web storage is part of HTML5's specification, but the draft and architecture for it has become so large that it is being split into its own specification, independent of HTML5.

Getting started with WURFL (Intermediate)

In this section, we start looking at device detection using the WURFL library from ScientiaMobile.

Previously, we looked at feature detection with the Modernizr library, so you may be asking why do we need to perform device detection as well. Simply put, both complement each other perfectly. For example, let's say we have a special version of the website that is fully optimized for the iPad; we can use WURFL to query the device's web browser and then see if the device is an iPad. If it is, we could then send the user to the optimized version.

Getting ready

We will be using ScientiaMobile's cloud version of the WURFL library. You can create a free account at `https://www.scientiamobile.com/cloud`. This free account will suffice for this book, however, for a production environment, you will need a higher tiered account.

Follow along at `http://www.scientiamobile.com/wurflCloud/gettingStarted/` to get your account set up. Once you get your account created and API key generated, go to the Capabilities page at `https://www.scientiamobile.com/wurflCloud/accountCapabilities` and drag over `device_os` and `device_os_version` to the **Your Capabilities** section of the page. This will allow you to check these two capabilities for this topic. Make sure you download the PHP client from the **Download Client Code** link on the account page.

After you get the code downloaded, create a new PHP Project in Aptana Studio and add the downloaded files to the directory of the newly created project.

How to do it...

Follow these steps:

1. On `index.php` of our PHP Project, add the following code. Please note that you will need to use the API key from your account in order for this to work.

```php
<?php
// Include the WURFL Cloud Client
// You'll need to edit this path
require_once 'Client/Client.php';

// Create a configuration object
$config = new WurflCloud_Client_Config();

// Set your WURFL Cloud API Key
$config->api_key = 'xxxxxx:xxxxxxxxxxxxxxxxxxxxxxxxxxxxxxxx';

// Create the WURFL Cloud Client
$client = new WurflCloud_Client_Client($config);

// Detect your device
$client->detectDevice();

// Use the capabilities
echo "Operating System: " . $client->getDeviceCapability('device_
os') . "<br />";
echo "Operating System Version: " . $client-
>getDeviceCapability('device_os_version') . "<br />";
?>
```

2. To test this, you will need to open the URL up in a mobile browser. Once you do so, you should see something similar to the following screenshot:

How it works...

Let's take a look at the code and see what we did:

```
// Include the WURFL Cloud Client
// You'll need to edit this path
require_once 'Client/Client.php';

// Create a configuration object
$config = new WurflCloud_Client_Config();
Here we are loading in the WURFL Cloud Client library and creating the
initial config file.
// Set your WURFL Cloud API Key
$config->api_key = 'xxxxxx:xxxxxxxxxxxxxxxxxxxxxxxxxxxxxxxx';

// Create the WURFL Cloud Client
$client = new WurflCloud_Client_Client($config);
```

Here, we assigned your API key to the config class' `api_key property`. We then instantiated the `Client` class, passing it our `config` object.

```
// Detect your device
$client->detectDevice();

// Use the capabilities
echo "Operating System: " . $client->getDeviceCapability('device_os')
. "<br />";
echo "Operating System Version: " . $client-
>getDeviceCapability('device_os_version') . "<br />";
```

Now we are at the meat of the example. Here, we are executing the `Client` method `detectDevice()` to start the `WURFL` querying process. Next, we are echoing back to the screen, that is, the results of our capability query for `device_os` and `device_os_version`. Pretty simple and straightforward, isn't it?

There's more...

With the free cloud account, we are limited to only looking at two device capabilities at a time. The good news is, we can change those out when we move to the next section. Again, if you plan on using this in a production environment, upgrade to one of the higher tiers, so you will have access to more capabilities and overall detections.

Alternative to ScientiaMobile's cloud

You can still use the standard WURFL library from `http://wurfl.sourceforge.net/`; however, there are licensing restrictions on it now. You may only use the open source version for open sourced projects and must follow the AGPL. You can also use it for evaluation purposes and then buy a license when ready for production.

Firefox user-agent trick

You can use Firefox to fake a mobile user-agent, eliminating the need to view the above code on a mobile device. To find out how to do this, have a look at `http://www.scientiamobile.com/wurflCloud/gettingStarted/`.

Using WURFL to check for Apple devices (Intermediate)

I'm sure, at some point you will have visited a website on your iPhone, iPod Touch, or even iPad and seen a full screen banner appear telling you that you should use the website's app in the App Store instead of the actual website.

In this topic, I am going to show you how you could do that using WURFL, and in the process, use Apple's Smart Banner approach for displaying app banners on a website.

Getting ready

The first thing we need to do is go back to our ScientiaMobile Cloud account and change the device capabilities we are going to use for this topic. Once you log on to your account, go to the **Capabilities** page and follow these directions:

▸ Drag the two capabilities we previously used to the **Trash** button, discarding them from your account

▸ Drag over the `brand_name` and `model_name` capabilities to your **Capabilities** section

Now that we have the capabilities we want to use, let's start writing some code. Create a new PHP Project in Aptana Studio to use.

How to do it...

Follow these steps:

1. Open up the `index.php` file that was created by Aptana Studio and add the following code:

   ```php
   <?php
   // Include the WURFL Cloud Client
   // You'll need to edit this path
   ```

```php
require_once 'Client/Client.php';

// Create a configuration object
$config = new WurflCloud_Client_Config();

// Set your WURFL Cloud API Key
$config->api_key = '357280:gSusq6nAaYNoUGZm0xVcEvfi3421LwOy';

// Create the WURFL Cloud Client
$client = new WurflCloud_Client_Client($config);

// Detect your device
$client->detectDevice();

?>
<!DOCTYPE html>
<html lang="en">
<head>
<meta charset=utf-8>
<meta name="viewport" content="width=device-width" />
<title>iOS Detection</title>
<body>
  <?php
    if ($client->getDeviceCapability('brand_name')=='Apple')
    {
       echo "<meta name='apple-itunes-app' content='app-id=375380948'>";
    }
    else
    {
       echo "You're not using an iOS device";
    }
  ?>
</body>
</html>
```

2. Now go to this page with Safari on your iOS device, and you should see the following screenshot:

Pretty nifty, isn't it? Clicking this banner will take the visitor straight to your app in the App Store, or they can simply click on the **X** to close the banner.

How it works...

The first part of the code is the same code we used to load our WURFL config and client objects, so let's skip to the next piece:

```
<!DOCTYPE html>
<html lang="en">
<head>
<meta charset=utf-8>
<meta name="viewport" content="width=device-width" />
<title>iOS Detection</title>
<body>
  <?php
    if ($client->getDeviceCapability('brand_name')=='Apple')
    {
      echo "<meta name='apple-itunes-app' content='app-
id=375380948'>";
    }
    else
    {
      echo "You're not using an iOS device";
    }
  ?>
</body>
</html>
```

The first part of this snippet is just standard HTML you would find on most pages; in the <body> statement, we have another PHP block. This if statement executes a device query to see if brand_name equals Apple. This covers the iPhone, iPod Touch, and iPad lines. Now <meta name='apple-itunes-app' content='app-id=375380948'> may look new. This is a meta tag the Safari on all iOS devices running iOS 6 or higher understands and uses it to show the smart banner that we generated.

There's more...

What if you have an app for the iPhone and a different app for the iPad? This is where the model_name capability we added comes into play. You can expand your if statement to do a check such as getDeviceCapability('model_name')=='iPad' and then change <meta name='apple-itunes-app'...> to reflect a different app for both the iPhone and iPad.

Chrome on iOS

If you visited your site using Chrome on iOS or on a device not running iOS 6, you've probably seen just a blank page and not even a **You're not using an iOS device** message. This is because you still passed the WURFL check we used in our `if` statement. You are on an Apple device, and that's all we've checked for. This meta tag will only work on iOS 6 Safari. So, how do you handle Chrome or devices such as pre-iOS 6? You could expand your `if` statement to check the browser to see if it is Safari (by checking `mobile_browser`), and if it isn't, display a standard image or banner with a link to your app. The same goes for checking for iOS 6 with the `device_os_version` check.

Apple app banners

To find out more information about this banner, visit the Apple Developer site at `http://developer.apple.com/library/ios/#documentation/AppleApplications/Reference/SafariWebContent/PromotingAppswithAppBanners/PromotingAppswithAppBanners.html`. Here, you can see how to generate banners for your app and more information about some additional properties you can add.

Beginning responsive design with PHP (Simple)

So far we have learned the basics of responsive web design, how to use Modernizr to perform feature detection, and then how to use `WURFL` to perform device detection. Let's start putting it all together with our favorite server-side language, PHP.

The page we are going to build is just a simple page that will serve as a landing page for our fictional consulting company, ACME Code Consulting. It will have a header image, some content that will explain our services, and then a web form the user can fill out to request more information.

Getting ready

Open the Aptana Studio project we created in the second topic; we will use it for the rest of the book and expand on it as we go.

How to do it...

We need to do a few things to get our project:

1. Copy over your WURFL code that has been used in the last few projects into the `wurfl` folder in this project.
2. Copy over the Modernizr JavaScript file as well from our previous Modernizr project.

3. Go to your ScientiaMobile Cloud account and change our capabilities to `is_mobile` and `is_tablet`.

4. We will also need a few more files in our project to start really getting our skeleton system together. Create the files as needed that appear in the following screenshot:

 The image in the images folder can be grabbed from the code download for this book.

5. Go ahead and open up `includes/header.inc` and add the following code:

```
<!doctype html>
<html>
<head>
<meta charset="utf-8">
<title>ACME Code Consulting</title>
<?php include ("includes/wurfl_client.inc"); ?>
<meta name="viewport" content="width=device-width; initial-scale=1.0; maximum-scale=1.0; user-scalable=0;" />
<link href="css/main.css" rel="stylesheet" type="text/css">
<script src="js/modernizr-latest.js" type="text/javascript"></script>
</head>
<body>
<div class="container">
   <div class="header"><img src="images/acme.png" alt="ACME Code Consultants" name="logo"/></a></div>
   <div class="sidebar">
     <ul class="nav">
       <li><a href="#">About Us</a></li>
```

```
        <li><a href="#">Our Clients</a></li>
        <li><a href="#">Privacy Policy</a></li>
        <li><a href="#">Client Login</a></li>
      </ul>
    </div>
```

6. Here, we are also calling `includes/wurfl_client.inc`, so go ahead and open it up and add the following:

```php
<?php
// Include the WURFL Cloud Client
// You'll need to edit this path
require_once './WURFL/Client/Client.php';

// Create a configuration object
$config = new WurflCloud_Client_Config();

// Set your WURFL Cloud API Key
$config->api_key = '';

// Create the WURFL Cloud Client
$client = new WurflCloud_Client_Client($config);

// Detect your device
$client->detectDevice();

?>
```

7. Again add in your WURFL Cloud API key, where it is needed. For now, our `index.php` file looks like the following code snippet:

```php
<?php include("includes/header.inc"); ?>
  <div class="content">
    <h1>Welcome!</h1>
    <p>Welcome to the home page of ACME Code Consultants where we
"write the code so you don't have to". We specialize in website
development,
      mobile development, business app development and we'll even
just look at the code you wrote and offer some suggestions if you
want!</p>
    <p>If you have any questions, feel free to contact us using
the form below</p>
  </div>
  </div>
</body>
</html>
```

In the next section, we will look at the CSS files and what they contain. Also, we will be adding more to these folders and files, as we continue on to seeing RESS in action.

How it works...

We are not really doing anything here that should be new to you. We are simply separating out some of our PHP code, so it is easier to manage. We are keeping our WURFL code in its own file so that it looks cleaner, and if we need to use it on multiple pages, it's best to have it in one file and simply include it in.

Laying out our page with RESS (Intermediate)

In this section, we will start laying out our pages based on the device that is viewing the site. We will use WURFL to assist us in determining which site to serve the visitor and then use PHP to serve up the site. Also, it will all be done through the same URL instead of redirecting them to a mobile version of the site.

Getting ready

We will use the same Aptana Studio project we worked with in the last section.

How to do it...

The first thing we need to do is set up our CSS files. We will have three files: `mobile.css` for our phones, `tablet.css` for our tablet devices, and then `main.css` for desktop/laptop devices. We will also have a fourth CSS file that will handle our colors and is universal across all the devices; this file will be named `style.css`. Follow these steps:

1. Let's start with `mobile.css`. This is what the contents will look like:

```
.container {
  width: 100%;
  background-color: #FFF;
  margin: 0px;
}
.header {
  background-color: #000;
}
.sidebar {
  background-color: #EADCAE;
}
```

```
.footer {
  background-color: #CCC49F;
  position: relative;
  clear: both;
}
```

2. This gives us a page geared towards most mobile screen sizes of 320 pixels. Now for our tablet stylesheet, follow this cope snippet:

```
.container {
  width: 768px;
  background-color: #FFF;
  margin: 0 auto;
}
.header {
  background-color: #000;
}
.sidebar {
  float: right;
  width: 180px;
  background-color: #EADCAE;
}
.content {
  padding: 10px 0;
  width: 588px;
  float: right;
}
.footer {
  padding: 10px 0;
  background-color: #CCC49F;
  position: relative;
  clear: both;
}
```

3. For the most part, this is the exact same code as `mobile.css`, just with different sizes for our content areas. And, finally, here is our `main.css` for our non-mobile devices:

```
.container {
  width: 960px;
  background-color: #FFF;
  margin: 0 auto;
}

.header {
```

```
    background-color: #000;
}

.sidebar {
  float: right;
  width: 180px;
  background-color: #EADCAE;
}

.content {

  padding: 10px 0;
  width: 780px;
  float: right;
}

.footer {
  padding: 10px 0;
  background-color: #CCC49F;
  position: relative;
  clear: both;
}
```

4. So, now that we have our three CSS files, you may be asking yourself how are we going to use these and where are the media queries? This is where PHP comes in. In our `header.inc` file, right after our `include` statement, for our WURFL file, add the following code:

```
if($client->getDeviceCapability('is_tablet'))
{
   $stylesheet = "tablet.css";

}
elseif($client->getDeviceCapability('is_mobile'))
{
   $stylesheet = "mobile.css";
}
else
{
   $stylesheet = "main.css";
}
```

Now, if you view the site on a mobile device, you should see a mobile version and then the tablet, and desktop/laptop version should look almost the same, except for the image, which will be dealt with in the next section.

How it works...

Refer to the following code snippet:

```
if($client->getDeviceCapability('is_tablet'))
{
  $stylesheet = "tablet.css";

}
elseif($client->getDeviceCapability('is_mobile'))
{
  $stylesheet = "mobile.css";
}
else
{
  $stylesheet = "main.css";
}
```

We are performing a WURFL device query to see if our device is first a tablet, and then if it is a mobile device and if neither are true, we load our default `.css` file. One note here: we are checking for the tablet device first, because it is technically a mobile device as well. So, if we do our mobile check first, it will be true and then load the `mobile.css` file, which, of course, won't look right on our tablet.

There's more...

You could also check the device width and gear your CSS files towards that. You will notice that on this basic example, there is no support for different device orientations, only portrait. You would add this in as well. It is a great learning exercise!

Displaying images (Intermediate)

When you viewed the previous code on your phone, you probably noticed that the image wasn't very mobile friendly. The same could even be said about the tablet version. How can we fix that as well? There are several ways we could fix this. We could use some client-side code such as JavaScript or CSS to scale them down to an appropriate size. The only problem with that is that by doing it client-side, you are losing performance and efficiency. What about resizing the images with PHP? That is certainly an option by using the GD or ImageMagick libraries and extensions in PHP. Again though there is a performance issue to consider, not to mention resizing any image could cause the quality of it to be lost or make it difficult to fully see.

Well, if we're not going to rescale them on the client or server side, then how are we going to display the images? Easy, we're going to cheat and simply load the version of the image that each device should see. Yes, that means you would have multiple versions of each image, but on the other hand, each device would see an image that was properly created and sized just for it.

Getting ready

Open the Aptana Studio project we have been using for the last few sections. Copy over the image folder from the code download, so you will have the new header images; you should have three total images: `acme.png`, `acme-320.png`, and `acme-768.png`.

How to do it...

Follow these steps:

1. We are going to leverage some of the code we used in the previous section to dynamically assign our header image to each device. Open up `header.inc` again and let's look at the code we just added. Make the highlighted changes:

```php
<?php
include ("includes/wurfl_client.inc");

if($client->getDeviceCapability('is_tablet'))
{
  $stylesheet = "tablet.css";
  $logo = "acme-768.png";
}
elseif($client->getDeviceCapability('is_mobile'))
{
  $stylesheet = "mobile.css";
  $logo = "acme-320.png";
}
else
{
  $stylesheet = "main.css";
  $logo = "acme.png";
}
?>
```

2. So now that we have our `$logo` variable assigned, let's put it to use. We will need to modify our `<div class="header">` section to look as follows:

```
<div class="header"><img src="images/<?php echo $logo; ?>"
alt="ACME Code Consultants" name="logo" style="max-width:100%"/></
a></div>
```

Now if you look at our progress so far, you will see a properly formatted header image displaying correctly on whatever device you use.

How it works...

The lines, `$logo = "acme-320.png"`, in each one of our device queries and assigns the filename of the proper header image that is sized correctly for the particular device. We then make sure that the image gets displayed by using the following code:

```
<img src="images/<?php echo $logo; ?>" alt="ACME Code Consultants"
name="logo" style="max-width:100%"/>
```

It just a normal HTML `img` call, but we have the `src` attribute that is equal to the assigned PHP variable.

There's more...

If performance isn't that much of a concern and you'd rather use PHP's ImageMagick or GD libraries to dynamically resize the images, please feel free to do so. I do, however, recommend ImageMagick over GD, and due to this, I use fewer server resources. The downfall though is that you may not find as many examples and documentation online to get up and going.

Getting visitor feedback (Advanced)

In this section, we display a form that the visitor can fill out to request more information about our services. We will also use another good component of RESS, loading in different content areas based on the device. So, with this, it will display two forms, one geared towards mobile devices and then one that will display on the tablet and desktop/laptop version.

Getting ready

If it is closed, open up your Aptana Studio project. We will need to modify our `header.inc` file again as well as create two new files. One will hold the mobile version of our form and the other will hold the full version of the form (which will also fit the tablet version pretty well). We will have two versions of the form, one with labels for our tablet/non-mobile devices and then one that does not use labels but instead uses the HTML5 form element of the placeholder.

How to do it...

Follow these steps:

1. Create two new files named `form_normal.html` and `form_mobile.html` and place them in the root directory of our project. Also, copy the `main.css`, `mobile.css`, and `tablet.css` files from the code download for the final project. Let's put some code in `form_normal.html`:

```html
<form id="contact">
  <fieldset>
    <legend>Contact Us!</legend>
    <ol>
      <li>
        <label for=name>Name</label>
        <input id=name name=name type=text required autofocus>
      </li>
      <li>
        <label for=email>Email</label>
        <input id=email name=email type=email required>
      </li>
      <li>
        <label for=phone>Phone</label>
        <input id=phone name=phone type=tel required>
      </li>
      <li>
        <label for=question>Question</label>
        <textarea id=question name=question rows=5 required></textarea>
      </li>
    </ol>
  </fieldset>
  <fieldset>
    <button type=submit>Submit</button>
  </fieldset>
</form>
```

2. Just a simple form with a few input fields, `textarea` and `label`; we are using HTML5's required field to make all these fields be required. This is a great addition to HTML5. Let's create our mobile form now. Open up `form_mobile.html` and place the following code there:

```html
<form id="contact">
  <fieldset>
    <ol>
      <li>
        <input id=name name=name type=text required autofocus placeholder="Name">
```

```
        </li>
        <li>
          <input id=email name=email type=email required
    placeholder="Email Address">
        </li>
        <li>
          <input id=phone name=phone type=tel required
    placeholder="Telephone">
        </li>
        <li>
          <textarea id=question name=question rows=5 required
    placeholder="Your Question"></textarea>
        </li>
      </ol>
    </fieldset>
    <fieldset>
      <button type=submit>Contact Us</button>
    </fieldset>
  </form>
```

It is almost the same form; we just do not have any form labels. We are dropping them in favor of the placeholder HTML5 element that helps us save some space and look a little more appealing.

3. Okay, now that we have two forms in two different files, how are we going to load them? Well, we will upload the same way we've been loading everything else in. Let's modify our `header.inc` file again. Make the following changes:

```php
<?php
include ("includes/wurfl_client.inc");


if($client->getDeviceCapability('is_tablet'))
{
  $stylesheet = "tablet.css";
  $logo = "acme-768.png";
  $form = "form_normal.html";
}
elseif($client->getDeviceCapability('is_mobile'))
{
  $stylesheet = "mobile.css";
  $logo = "acme-320.png";
  $form = "form_mobile.html";
}
else
{
  $stylesheet = "main.css";
```

```
    $logo = "acme.png";
    $form = "form_normal.html";
}
?>
```

Again we are using the same form for the non-mobile devices and the tablet device. The CSS will be different to account for the screen size differences.

4. Now to actually load in our form, open `index.php` and add the following code right after the closing paragraph tag:

```
<?php include ($form); ?>
```

Was that simple enough? Now check your devices, and you should see the form displayed; it appears different on your phone and desktop/laptop.

How it works...

We are using the same functionality we previously used to load in the form dynamically:

```
$form = "form_normal.html";
```

We are assigning the form filename to the device through our WURFL code blocks just like we did in the header image and then in the CSS file.

```
<?php include ($form); ?>
```

Here, we are just using the standard PHP `include` function to load in our form based on the variable.

There's more...

This was a great example to show how you can use RESS ideas to load in content based on the device. You could have advertising on your main site, but when it is seen on a mobile device, you might load in advertising that looks more like what mobile users see in apps.

You could also use this to load in Flash content that wouldn't work on a mobile website but works perfectly on the main website. Again, all this is served through one URL.

Wrapping it up (Simple)

Quite a ride it has been, hasn't it? We have touched briefly on several subjects in this book, and I hope you have enough of a basis to start using RESS in your own projects. There are several other ways you can implement some of the items we did here in this book. Let's add one other feature to our site; let' get the user's location so that way we can see where our visitors are coming from and open an office in an area that has a lot of interest.

Getting ready

We have already done this before when we were getting started with Modernizr, but let's take it step by step again. Open up your Aptana Studio project one last time.

How to do it...

Follow these steps:

1. We need to make one final edit to our `header.inc` file. Open it up and add the following code:

```
<script src="js/modernizr-latest.js" type="text/javascript"></
script>
    <script type="text/javascript">
      function findMe()
      {
        var geoService = navigator.geolocation;
        if (Modernizr.geolocation) {
          alert("We would like to know your location for future
growth.");
            navigator.geolocation.getCurrentPosition(showCurrentLoca
tion, errorHandler, {
              enableHighAccuracy : true
            });
        } else {
          alert("Your Browser does not support Geolocation.");
        }
      }

      function showCurrentLocation(position)
      {
        document.getElementById("curlocation").innerHTML =
"Current Latitude : " + position.coords.latitude + " , Current
Longitude : " + position.coords.longitude;
      }

      function errorHandler(error)
      {
        alert("Error while retrieving current position. Error
code: " + error.code + ",Message: " + error.message);
      }
    </script>
```

2. This should all look familiar from our previous project. Now, let's load it up. Previously, we required the user to click on a button, this time around we will have it happen automatically. Still in `header.inc`, change your body tag to look like the following code:

```
<body onLoad="findMe()">
```

Now when you go to the site, you should see the pop up telling the user the reason for tracking the location.

How it works...

Again this is the same code we previously used; the only difference this time is as follows:

```
<body onLoad="findMe()">
```

As soon as the page loads, this executes our JavaScript function `findMe()` to prompt the user about the tracking and to get the actual location. We would then write this to a server log or database, so we could run metrics on where our visitors are coming from.

There's more...

Well, that's it. Our pages should look like the following screenshot on our computer:

And on a phone, it will look like the following screenshot:

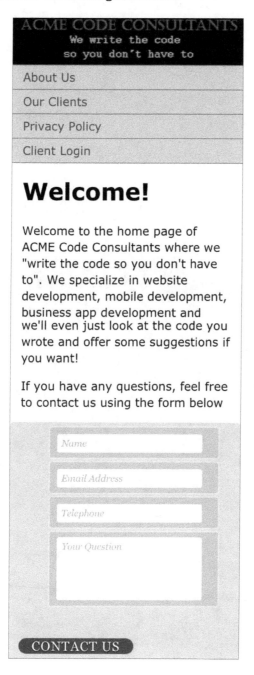

Thank you for following along, and I hope you had as much fun reading this as I did writing it!

Thank you for buying
Instant RESS Implementation How-to

About Packt Publishing

Packt, pronounced 'packed', published its first book "*Mastering phpMyAdmin for Effective MySQL Management*" in April 2004 and subsequently continued to specialize in publishing highly focused books on specific technologies and solutions.

Our books and publications share the experiences of your fellow IT professionals in adapting and customizing today's systems, applications, and frameworks. Our solution based books give you the knowledge and power to customize the software and technologies you're using to get the job done. Packt books are more specific and less general than the IT books you have seen in the past. Our unique business model allows us to bring you more focused information, giving you more of what you need to know, and less of what you don't.

Packt is a modern, yet unique publishing company, which focuses on producing quality, cutting-edge books for communities of developers, administrators, and newbies alike. For more information, please visit our website: www.packtpub.com.

Writing for Packt

We welcome all inquiries from people who are interested in authoring. Book proposals should be sent to author@packtpub.com. If your book idea is still at an early stage and you would like to discuss it first before writing a formal book proposal, contact us; one of our commissioning editors will get in touch with you.

We're not just looking for published authors; if you have strong technical skills but no writing experience, our experienced editors can help you develop a writing career, or simply get some additional reward for your expertise.

Responsive Web Design with HTML5 and CSS3

ISBN: 978-1-84969-318-9   Paperback: 324 pages

Learn responsive design using HTML5 and CSS3 to adapt websites to any browser or screen size

1. Everything needed to code websites in HTML5 and CSS3 that are responsive to every device or screen size

2. Learn the main new features of HTML5 and use CSS3's stunning new capabilities including animations, transitions and transformations

3. Real world examples show how to progressively enhance a responsive design while providing fall backs for older browsers

jQuery Mobile Web Development Essentials

ISBN: 978-1-84951-726-3   Paperback: 246 pages

Learn to use the touch-optimized, cross-device, cross-platform jQM web framework for smartphones and tablets

1. Create websites that work beautifully on a wide range of mobile devices with jQuery mobile

2. Learn to prepare your jQuery mobile project by learning through three sample applications

3. Packed with easy to follow examples and clear explanations of how to easily build mobile-optimized websites

Please check **www.PacktPub.com** for information on our titles

HTML5 Canvas
Cookbook

Over 80 recipes to revolutionize the web experience with
HTML5 Canvas

Eric Rowell

HTML5 Canvas Cookbook

ISBN: 978-1-84969-136-9   Paperback: 348 pages

Over 80 recipes to revolutionize the web experience with
HTML5 Canvas

1. The quickest way to get up to speed with HTML5
    Canvas application and game development

2. Create stunning 3D visualizations and games
    without Flash

3. Written in a modern, unobtrusive, and objected
    oriented JavaScript style so that the code can be
    reused in your own applications.

4. Part of Packt's Cookbook series: Each recipe is
    a carefully organized sequence of instructions to
    complete the task as efficiently as possible

Dreamweaver CS5.5 Mobile and
Web Development with HTML5,
CSS3, and jQuery

Harness the cutting edge features of Dreamweaver for mobile and
web development

David Karlins   PACKT

Dreamweaver CS5.5 Mobile and Web Development with HTML5, CSS3, and jQuery

ISBN: 978-1-84969-158-1   Paperback: 284 pages

Harness the cutting edge features of Dreamweaver for
mobile and web development

1. Create web pages in Dreamweaver using the
    latest technology and approach

2. Add multimedia and interactivity to your websites

3. Optimize your websites for a wide range
    of platforms and build mobile apps with
    Dreamweaver

Please check **www.PacktPub.com** for information on our titles